Driving With My Blinker On

Eleanor Wolfe Hoomes

A

Vabella Publishing
P.O. Box 1052
Carrollton, Georgia 30112
www.vabella.com

Cover design by Diana Black, Diana Designs

Manufactured in the United States of America

13-digit ISBN   978-1-938230-21-9

Library of Congress Control Number: 2012953303

10 9 8 7 6 5 4 3 2 1

For

Opal Wolfe, my mother
Angelia Hoomes, my daughter
Victoria Jordan, my granddaughter

Other Volumes of Poetry

By

Eleanor Wolfe Hoomes

BREAD AND ROSES, TOO
EYE OF THE BEHOLDER
GREEN THUMBS

The above books are available in soft cover and e-book from Barnes and Noble, Amazon or directly from Vabella publishing.

Visit eleanorwolfehoomes.com for more details.

TABLE OF CONTENTS

THREE

FOUR

FIVE

ONE

Poetry doesn't have to be deep;
it doesn't have to make me weep;
it doesn't even have to rhyme,
but if it doesn't seize my heart,
twist my soul, frission my brain,
or punch me in the gut,
it must tickle my funny bone,
and, at least, compel me
to smile in recognition
or laugh until my sides ache
at the absurdity
of the human condition.

DRIVING WITH MY BLINKER ON

She reclined in the shotgun seat, feet propped
on the windshield, long legs bypassing the
dash, her swimmer's blonde hair serving as

blinders to her face and eyes. Ear buds pelted
her with music; occasionally she sang along
in her pitch-perfect soprano. Her thumbs

were busy texting, but when there was a lull,
she slept. After I merged from Riverside Drive
onto I-75, she roused long enough to say,

"Gran, you're driving with your blinker on."
She'd been accepted by the only college to
which she'd applied. So many changes,

challenges, options faced her. I wanted to
warn her about predatory boys, wild frat
parties, drugs, alcohol. I wanted to advise her

about academic choices, internships, work.
I wanted to know about her friends, school
extra-curricular activities, dreams. I wanted

her to tender me her secrets as she had
once thrust bouquets of uprooted zinnias
into my welcoming hands. I had a

reliable web-site on birth control I wanted
to give her. I wanted to talk to her about
the "morning after" pill, date rape, staying

safe. I wanted to know she was ready to launch herself into the world, but even when I changed lanes just in time for a

road gator to attack the front of my Sonata, to the tune of $450, all she said was, "Gran, you really need to turn off your blinker."

OPAL, WOMAN OF THE SOUTH

The amulet of beauty, expected to ward off
loss, that promised extended performances
in emerald arenas, has tarnished and
is developing the patina of antiquity.

"I'm pretty as a doll.   Take my picture."

Naomi, handmaidened by aging Ruths
attending her with cobwebbed patience
and acid wine, fumbles with a turnstile,
bewildered by its balky rotations.

"Don't cancel my lunch reservations."

Her senses, once docile, obedient, have
been ambushed by clotted perspectives
like just-hatched baby turtles rushing
the wrong way toward security lights.

"I lived in cotton fields and orange groves."

Memories– of parents, siblings, church,
of being a beautiful bride and mother and
being widowed too young– leak drip by
drip as sunlight grows dry and brittle.

"I'm a jewel, but I don't dance."

Memories– of moving, establishing a new
home, of changing work in midlife, and
becoming an artist– drip drop by drop
as twilight grows cold and hardens.

"I'm afraid I'll fall and break my hip."

On a pilgrimage to The Land of Advancing
Silence and Shifting Realities where no one
can follow, she wanders in cotton fields,
orange groves, and her own paintings.

"Did I really paint that picture?"

At nine o'clock on a July night when the
whip-poor-wills start calling, a memory
surfaces from an underworld labyrinth
as she looks at her great granddaughter.

"I think I used to be as tall as you are."

The whip-poor-wills finish their songs.
Her sieved memory side steps, and reality
grows thinner as the Chisel of Time
chips opals, dimming their fire.

"Now, tell me just who you are."

FERTILE FIELDS

Dawn's Bright Eye welcomes me
to a day as mutable as a cumulus
cloud where everything is new
and where everything is old.

I join those who are still listed
in the "Book of the Living"
to shop in the emporiums
of the land, the sky, the sea,

where the essentials of life,
dreams lush as moss and molten
as magma, have no price tags–
they're free for the dreaming,

and where I become what I
select at no charge and plant
in my own fertile fields.
Unto dark–

when the Night cares not whether
I sleep in linen or silk or cotton–
or nothing–
as long as I dream.

THE AVENUE

I wait until the light loses its grip
and the rounded moon comes calling
to gather into my arms
all the bustle of The Avenue
where there are no barriers, no sharp edges,
where my ears are filled with warm words,
where I am less alone,
listening as each story begins and unfolds.

Like a runaway grocery cart
in a sloping parking lot,
I careened from fender to fender
until I crashed into you and
we came to rest on The Avenue,
sharing this abode we built together.
This is where we heal each other,
where our windows are lit with candles.

Stranger, what are you concealing
with no lit candles in your windows
and your handcuffs of despair?
Welcome to The Avenue.   Come in.
Is the wine sweet enough for you?
Share your story and we'll share ours,
let them unfold in a journey of warm words
as moon and candles illuminate the way.

In the creeping light of dawn
the candles are burning low, but for now
The Avenue has worked its magic.
No longer a stranger, you have escaped
your handcuffs of anguish–
and so have we– at least for one night
of moonlight, burning candles,
hearing hearts and healing words.

TO SLEEP, TO DREAM

And on the eighth day God says:
      Let my people dream
      because dreams mean nothing
      and dreams mean everything.

So as light ebbs, God's people withdraw
to caves and castles, huts and hovels,
igloos and tents, condos and cottages,
mansions and shotgun houses. God's people

evade the maddening moonlight with brown
river reeds and invading lamp light with
blackout screens and in ebony linen shadows
lie down to sleep, to dream in symbols of

living Technicolor. The majority of the
people do not esteem their stuttering, iconic
dreams, and remember upon waking that
dreams mean nothing and forget that dreams

mean everything.   But a few night-time
dreamers upon waking, remember that the
emblematic and eternal flashing symbols
both mean nothing and everything,

and thus find themselves awake and
dreaming, and their dreams take shapes,
so the dreamers give them names
as they discover and create new realities.

And the world turns 'round and again
God's people, maddening moonlight
thwarted by blackout screens, lie down in
ebony linen shadows, to sleep, to dream.

And God says:
      A few will be enough.
      Maybe.

LET THERE BE LIGHT

God looked out across her domain and said,
"By Hera," a sly dig at her coming Greek
competitor, "compared to the light the dark
is vast." God thought about this discrepancy,
and then she said, "Let there be light."
So for daylight she lit the sun, and then
to take the edge off the black of night, she
lit the stars, and to make things even more
interesting, she lit the moon in phases.

At first humans worked and played during
daylight hours and rested and slept during
the dark of night, but soon people noted
that less sleep was needed during the
full phase of the moon. Some humans
mused, "If some light is good, more would
be better." Then came the discoveries—
fire, candles, whale oil, gas, electricity,
and solar power. And thus humans began
to light cities and then country sides.
Children whined for night lights to keep
the monsters at bay. Even God shuddered
at all those gaudy displays of Christmas
lights. People developed insomnia, so they
took sleeping pills, used black-out masks
and drapes, attended sleep disorder clinics,
and needed afternoon naps.

The earth became a spinning sphere of
lights. Light spilt into the heavens and was
reflected back to earth, accelerating the
slow warming process of the earth itself.

God looked down, shook her head in sorrow,
and said, "Just look at those sorry fools
on earth turning their nights into days.
By Hera," even though Hera was now just
part of Greek mythology, God held onto
old habits, "Why did I give them free will?
I gave them night so they could sleep."

And then–
God heaved a hurricane-sized sigh.

IN MY FAVORITE FANTASY

Wearing a green silk dancing frock,
emerald rings, and silver slippers,
I waltz into the heavens, a seeker
of answers, attempting to converse
with the Big Boss in rhymed verse.

"Is human life a practical joke,
like an ant farm or a zoo,
designed to amuse you while you
cope with your own immortality
and come to terms with eternity?"

A rhythm of silence, curving down
like breaking waves, engulfs me,
giving me new insights into the
passive-aggressive possibility
of celestial taciturnity.

ETERNITY

"Where will you spend eternity?" asks
the electric sign at New Hope Church.
My writer's brain, accustomed to
composing beginnings, middles, and
ends, boggles at the infinity of eternity.

My life is finite.   Like my writing,
there was a beginning; I am in the
middle, and there will be an end.
The expected answer is "Heaven,"
but a place without the spice of sin,
sounds humdrum, monotonous,
tedious, and insipid as gelatin.

However, the Garden of Eden with its
absence of sin–?   No?   An alternate
to New Hope Church's idea of eternity
could be Nature's Mobius Strip, forever
twisting in and out, over and under,
where the full spectrum, souls as well
as bodies, are recycled ad infinitum.

Thus I would like to spend eternity
in a Southern Forest where my ashes
would enrich the soil hosting
hearts-a-bustin', native azaleas,
jessamine, cinnamon ferns, chanterelles,
may apples, and oakleaf hydrangeas, my
spirit dwelling in a Carolina silver bell.

When the Carolina silver bell finally
topples in a spring storm, my spirit could
flit over to a sweet bay magnolia tree,
and I would be happy to continue on
Nature's Mobius Strip throughout eternity–

TROUBLE

Emerging from Morpheus's Domain
where dreams and insanity abide side
by side, I can taste the bile of Trouble's
menace.   An assassin lurking in the
charcoal shadows preceding dawn,
he is moving into position to snatch
serenity from my locked pockets.

I cannot pinpoint his exact location,
but I sense Trouble stalking around me,
primed for mayhem, moving closer with
each orbit, twirling a copperhead in one
hand and a poison ivy vine in the other.
Heart pounding, peripheral vision useless,
defensive strategies worthless, I pivot
clockwise straining to pinpoint Trouble.

Trouble swaggers from the shadows,
clad in black leather, cigarette dangling
from the corner of his mouth, ebony hair
slicked back, no copperhead, no poison
ivy vine, but oozing nuclear threat,
nonetheless.   He sneers at my impotence.
"I'm about to smash your Pandora's
Box.   I'm just giving you a heads up.
Yeah, like that will do you any good."

His mission accomplished, he struts
back into the fading shadows, having
assailed my belief that I have control
over my own destiny and having raised
my anxiety level to Code Red heights.

CRY ME A RIVER

"Cry me a river..."

We were no longer young, but I was very
foolish, risking all for you while you risked
nothing. You remained enshrouded in a forest

of shadows, permitting easy physical access
but denying the intimacy of self-revelation.
Sipping our martinis, we sat in a smoky haze,

dark and heavy with an atmosphere
of languor and decadence. Mass produced
antiqued mirrors reflected ghostly duplicates,

eerie doppelgangers, creating disorienting
suggestions of urban decay, the dark underbelly
of modern life, and moral ambiguity–

not Rick's Place in CASABLANCA, but
in my dreams we were Bogart and Bergman.
Bathed in a rose spotlight, a sultry blonde,

lush curves caressed by red satin, sang
torchy love songs in a rich, husky voice,
rough around the edges– honey and sand.

I pitched my voice just under the lyrics
to whisper, "She's singing our song."
You flicked ash from your cigarette.

Your face was etched by shadows in the
sputtering glow of candles. Seduced
by the forbidden, I saw a lean, imposing

figure, a man of mystery, dark hair lightly
silvered.   I envisioned myself as a femme
fatale starring in a neo film noir.

And then– you stubbed out your cigarette,
leaned across the candle-lit table and
with careless cruelty shattered

my middle-aged dreams when you tossed
me aside like last night's used condom
for a woman twenty years younger than I.

You stood and strolled away without a
backward glance, leaving me to pay the
tab and to plot my way back home.

"I cried a river over you..."

WAITING

For too long no redecorating has
occurred in the rooms of her heart,
the antique love prominent in the

center, the ancient grief filling the
corners, the bare walls waiting, her
sorrow vibrating like a tightly strung

wire from the front hall to the back
doorway while her threadbare life
waits—neatly folded on a chair.

A VANISHING BREED

Alas!   We Romantics are a vanishing breed.
Poet-writers, who should be speaking
to and for our endangered species, seduced
by the broad and easy, have abdicated.

Resolve wavering, gazes averted,
passion no longer pulsing within,
they have pacemakers installed just in case
they have an urge to write about love.

So love becomes an afterthought,
an accident to trip stumbling fools.
To fill the void left by their abdication,
they record in cramped, sparse hands

The monotony of real-time dramas
and publish (as told to...) the premature
dueling memoirs of callow youths
with lives yet to be lived, whose creed is:

"If we are paid obscene advances,
whatever we do is everybody's business."
Reader's coins are lost in the greedy maws
of the publishers' vending machines.

Alas!   We yearn for a mermaid's tale
spinning through the mind's vision,
cartwheeling perception into reality,
and riddles that are never about answers.

BREACHING BORDERS

After the writer-in-residence fills
the eraser board with red and green inks,
she continues writing on the white walls.

Surprised into attentiveness,
I admire the breached borders
and grab onto a metaphor–

ourselves, our minds
are surfaces for the application
of life's quick, rich inks.

While I rather despise the term,
"thinking outside the box,"
(after all, the box keeps us grounded and

from having to reinvent the metaphor)
red and green inks in the hands
of a writer breaching borders

is altogether another matter.

HEIR

Most of her possessions were recyclable,
the rest flammable.
The earth would never inherit her things.
She could hold her life in the palm
of her hand.

Where did she hide her dreams?
Dreams with no beginning date,
dreams with no ending date,
continuous dreams–
How many doors would I need
to open to share one of her dreams?

The dreams playing and
replaying inside her head,
making much ado about something,
could never be swept away
by floods or tornados,
could never be stolen by thieves
nor burned by arsonists,
could never be accessed by me,
could only be eroded by Time
and erased by Death.

At the end she folded into herself,
pulling her borders to the center.
She died still hoarding her dreams.
Having failed to find and open
a door to even one dream,
I bade her and my inheritance
a final farewell.

A ROAD DOES NOT GO THERE

He asks me the way to my heart.
I tell him a road does not go there.

And if it did, summer could not
melt the snow and ice.

And if it did, the sun could not
burn away the mist and fog.

And if it did—
I would not be there.

THE PIANO PLAYER

She leaves the beds unmade,
lets the dishes drain,
plays the piano and sings
country, jazz, classic, swing—

She leaves the floors unswept,
lets the dinner burn,
plays the piano and sings
gospel, blues, ragtime, pop—

She leaves the clothes unironed,
lets the water run,
plays the piano and sings
new age, soul, opera, rock.

But— her husband and children
just want to be fed,
always have clean clothes,
and fresh linens on their beds.

THE EX-PIANO PLAYER

No one mourned with her when the last note
faded.   No one cried with her when the music
died. She played the piano and sang– gospel,
blues, country, and rock– but her husband

and children just wanted to be fed, always
have clean clothes, and fresh linens on their
beds.   It was years– and eons too late–
before the drinkers of their own mismixed

elixir realized that when the music departed,
icicles formed on the ends of her fingers
and the tip of her tongue, broke off, and
piercing her heart, splintered and melted,

beginning the slow erosion, drip by
spondaic drip, of her soul and their hearth.

ON OUR SIXTIETH WEDDING ANNIVERSARY

I wore life like a prom corsage–
one day violets, another orchids–
but mostly sweetheart roses.

We made many promises to each
other and kept most of them.   How
could I have known how happy

I was wearing sweetheart roses,
untarnished by obscure shadows?
Today, on what would have been

our sixtieth wedding anniversary,
I sit in a cat-shredded club chair,
wedding ring loose on my finger.

Because we had such a good run,
I can't toss off the ring, discard it
as Life discarded you when Death

flicked his fickle wrist.   Now you
are no longer busy in another room.
The dogwoods are in bloom, and

I am a radiant bride, walking
toward you, toward us, carrying
a bouquet of sweetheart roses.

As I breathe in the memories, I
twist my thin wedding ring, and
I hear you busy in the next room.

SWALLOWTAILS, OH MY! AND MORE

"Gran, look.   I'm a butterfly princess!"
Yellow and black swallowtails cling to her arms;
red admirals light on her golden curls.
"Swallowtails, Oh My! And more," she whispers.

"Hold out your hands, Gran.   Don't move."
I bow.   "Yes, your Butterfly Highness."
"Shhh.   You'll scare them away.   Palms up."
We stand motionless, arms outstretched.

The wind teases our hair and clothes,
the leaves of the trees, the meadow grasses.
At first swallowtails and admirals tiptoe
over our fingers and the palms of our hands.

Their relatives– eastern tailed blues, emperors,
painted ladies, pearl crescents, fritillaries –
join them to explore our arms, shoulders, hair–
wings fluttering, antennae probing.

Then she laughs and twirls around and around.
"Fly!" she cries.   "Up, up, up to the sky!"
The butterflies ascend in clouds of black, gold,
yellow, orange, tan, white, lavender, and indigo.

"Like sparks, like kites, like balloons!"
She laughs and claps her hands as they scatter
into the aquamarine and pearl tinged air.
Clasped hands swinging, we continue walking

Through the wildflower meadow, ripe
with fragrances, surprises and promises.

ADVICE TO A GODDAUGHTER

You've been good too long, Girl;
Now it's your turn to spin your world.
Take a few chances, Love.
A life lived without risk is dull, dull, dull.

It's time you played hooky.
Shake off the shackles of your desk;
Drink two, or even three, mimosas, Love.
With no apology, savor that last cookie.

Showcase your body and face.
Slap on make-up, spray on perfume.
Exploit the allure of black lace, Love.
Give the boys something to chase.

Accept a date with that bad boy.
You don't want to marry him,
Just think of him as a pet, Love,
Or even a new wind-up toy.

Buy that red convertible Sebring.
Now you can splash in the puddles
And dance in the rain, Love.
Mama's no longer pulling your strings.

Bask in your new found feminine power,
Eliminate the concept of "If Only"
And "Almost" from your vocabulary, Love.
Live to the maximum each hour.

Now it's your turn.   It's true
You've been good too long, Girl.
Ask not for whom the world spins, Love,
Make it spin for you.

AERIAL MINUETS

Rebuffed by asphalt parking lots,
nourished by aromatic tapestries,
shedding a shy silence as you dip
into Nature's ample pockets,
Butterfly and Dragonfly, delicate,
incandescent ambassador cousins,
a duet winging prophecies, you are
glee bantering in slanted sunlight.

Your wings flash uncontested
as you translate the vertical,
making random consolations
less fragmentary, impinging
on my losses and regrets,
feeding unarticulated hungers.

I envy your aerial minuets.
Free and holy, untarnished by sin,
you will fall too soon.   You will
            pirouette,
        glide and dip,
      sidestep, falter,
            and drift
to earth in one brief season.

My existence is a mystic file
yellowing like antique lace.
I cannot evade indefinitely
the summons I hear; the sunset
licks the contracting horizon,
and I start to pirouette–

TWO

Yesterday I read a rhyming fairy tale,
set in a long ago time and a far away land,
about a beautiful princess in peril
and the brave hero who rescued her.
But– if I had woven the fairy tale, hereafter,
the hero would have been in peril, and
amid page-turning suspense and laughter,
the princess would have rescued him into
"Once upon a time" and "Happily ever after."

MISTLETOE

The open-house was over, and
everyone was gone but one.
She posed under the mistletoe.
The fire was banked, burning low.
She waited for their first kiss
under the white-berried mistletoe.
But– he smiled slow,
his eyes remote,
put on his hat and overcoat,
said, "Thank you for inviting me.
Merry Christmas.   Goodnight,"
opened the door and retreated
from the possibility of them
into the white
of the winter twilight.

Monday

An alarming duet of clamor and pain
rouses my senses, rattles my brain,
laying traps, fizzling out–

Snatch on clothes tossed over
the backs of chairs, slip on shoes
playing peek-a-boo at the top of the stairs–

The bread has gone stale, concrete almost,
milk, eggs, sugar, vanilla, butter–
Voila! bread pudding or French toast–

Unanswered and unreturned phone calls,
speed dial, silence, zero from that quarter,
face it– that romance is dead in the water–

Pull my bloodied heart from the hamper,
immerse it in a basin of Movin'-On,
guaranteed to cleanse stomped on love–

Even though my love proved fickle,
on Mondays I expect a better world.
After all, zero is just a blooming circle–

DON'T FIX ME UP

I am a woman currently living single–
by choice, thank you very much.
Yet, my close friends and distant relatives
keep pushing me to get out there and mingle.

"I know just the man you need to meet,"
a soon to be ex-friend greeted me.
"He's uneducated, but really smart,
younger than you, unemployed, really sweet."

"Not very good-looking, a little stout."
She paused, but not long enough.   "Short.
Balding.   Lives with his mama, but, I think,
the two of you would enjoy going out."

Now, I can find bald, undesirable,
unemployed, short and stout, mama boys
all by myself.   Why couldn't she find me
a tall, wealthy, and handsome possible?

But, if I am not very much mistaken–
and all evidence proves that I am not–
the complex, intelligent, employed men
are gay, commitment phobic, or taken.

I am a woman currently living single,
but for the right man I might agree
to mingle if he caused my heart to sing,
my toes to curl, and my brain to tingle.

APPLE MOMENT

He looked around the garden and smiled
at the temptations displayed there.
"Looks to me like I'm here to play awhile.
Thank you," he said to the recumbent serpent,
"for the apple, girl, and fig-leaf garment."

Indeed, the girl was unexpectedly dense
about the primary importance of those
protective rules designed for her defense.
She ignored the "Do not partake of" sign,
dined on the apple– Oh, it was divine!

Now we all know what became her fate–
exile, tears, and travail for the girl after
she partook of the apple, became his mate,
started a fashion trend in fig-leaf garments–
Oh, how she paid for their apple moment!

WITHOUT WORDS

The words by-passed them,
roaring past like fighter jets
flying faster than the speed of sound,
trailing silent contrails
and speechless sonic booms.

Left stranded, they dug
into their verbal arsenals
depleted by the heavy artillery
already launched at each other
and came up voiceless.

No amount of wanting, of wishing
gave voice to the words and phrases
needed to cross the no-man's land
widening between them,
needed to negotiate a cease-fire.

Without words
they could negotiate no truce.
Without words
they could negotiate no lasting peace.
Their world exploded in silence.

TIRED

With you I was too long lost in
the heady fervor of burning
words and searing kisses, of

lightning peaks and thundering
lows.   With you I was too long
enveloped in excesses of adrenalin

charged, unbridled passions,
leaping blindly from absolutes to
absolutes in an unplanned world

of high volume emotions.
Coveting an emotional range
less than an octave and a heart

fortified against invading passions,
I willingly paid the asking price
for freedom, for peace–

detached solitude in the
empty silence
of a heart without love.

THE ROMANCE WRITER

A curtain at a window on the second
story flutters.   The writer peers around
the edges with anticipation.   With shy

envy she watches her hero and heroine,
lovers dressed in early 19th Century
festive finery, as he lifts her gloved

hand and gently turns it over to kiss
the throbbing pulse on the inside of her
slender white wrist.   The writer wonders

when the love she so artfully depicts
will rap on her door.   When will love
present itself?   At what inconvenient

hour will love demand instant
admittance, brush past the dignified
butler, shove aside the handsome

footman, send the saucy parlor maid
reeling, and leap up the curving staircase,
crying his undying love all the way?

HIS BAGPIPES

Skirling bagpipes, fleeting glimpses of a kilt
and knobby knees, the stink of his cigar–
Damn!   His ghost haunts me.   The apparition
must have hellish knowledge of my sedition.

His stalking me is not part of my simply
designed and carefully executed plan.
I gave him my heart; he destroyed my life.
His death ended my life sentence as wife.

I dreamed; I schemed to liberate myself
from his evil regime; but now he taunts me.
I shiver in dread and fear that, after all,
he has solved the mystery of his fatal fall.

SCENARIO FOR A MODERN FAIRY TALE

Scene i

In a springtime, silver, seductive,
a Beautiful Girl meets a Handsome Boy.
The Girl beckons; the Boy pursues,
both blinded by passion.
In slow motion a reel unfurls,
laden with celluloid emotion–

Scene ii

Candlelight suppers, dances on moonlit
beaches, picnics in the park, frolics
with Frisbees and Golden Retrievers,
sheltering in each other's arms, cherishing
their love in common– summertime
happiness in fairy tale clichés.

Scene iii

Now flickering past in fast motion
the reds and golds of autumn,
rife with stock celluloid emotion–
faster, faster–
differences, disappointments,
petty spats, all that– and more–
seeing each other clearer and clearer
until their hearts finally accept
what their senses tell them.

Scene iv

The film segues into bleak winter
with a closeup of two sets
of diverging footsteps in the snow.
Now with clarity of reason, she
lives alone and unhappy for a season.

Epilogue

Until the next silver springtime,
when the Beautiful Girl meets another
Handsome Boy.   She beckons;
he pursues, both blinded by passion.
Laden with celluloid emotion,
a sequel unfurls in slow motion.

GOD'S EMISSARY

Fee, fie, foe, fum!
I smell the blood of a lone wo-man.
Be she brave or be she yellow,
I'll pierce her heart; I'm a strong fellow.

Fee, fie, foe, fum!
I smell the fear of a loose wo-man.
Be hair black or be it yellow,
I'll slit her throat; I'm a just fellow.

Fee, fie, foe, fum!
"Stand still, Witch-Bitch, don't you run.
Be you young or be you older,
You're mine now; my bloods boils colder."

Fee, fie, foe, fum!
I crave the cries of a scared wo-man.
Be it day or be it night,
I smite stray women; it's my right.

Fee, fie, foe, fum!
I smell the blood of my next vic-tim.

GOLD DIGGER

She spurns his proposal
when she learns
how little he earns.

She has broken the bough;
now no cradle will rock
in their wedded tree top.

Western forests may burn,
the earth may revolve
while humans devolve.

The Delta may flood,
a tornado may scramble
Luverne, Alabama.

Yet amid life's hullabaloos
her only concern
is how little he earns.

THEY HAVE VOWED TO CLEAVE

They have vowed to cleave only to each other
and then have exchanged rings.   They have
been pronounced husband and wife, have
kissed and walked down the aisle together.

The day, born in covetousness and fantasy,
began in delicate needles of moonlight
and the thrill of plucking the forbidden
from his best friend.   It has now degenerated
into self-conscious excesses, paid for by
the bride's father with a second mortgage.

No walls, no roofs can confine the revelry.
Amid the bray of drunken laughter generated
by bawdy toasts, raucous references
to wedding night acrobatics, and
lewd accolades aimed at the bride's ample
assets spilling over her virginal white
strapless wedding gown, the bride and
the groom twinkle and glide onto the dance
floor and begin their solo wedding waltz.

Soon the groom's eyes stray over his bride's
right shoulder, wandering from one bridal
attendant to another, searching for the tall
blonde former roommate of his bride.

Their eyes meet.   He winks and smiles an
invitation, but the road to her consent is
blocked by detour signs and dense fog.

Undaunted, his eyes move to the second,
where he is stalled by a STOP sign and
then on to the third to be halted by a
traffic light permanently glowing red.

The fourth bridal attendant has old scores
to settle with the bride.   When his eyes meet
hers, with a promising smile and a slight nod
of her head, she flashes him a green light.

Now sporting a Cheshire cat grin, he
whispers, "I love you," and with a kiss
he waltzes his bride into wedded bliss.

THE PERPETUATION OF THE SPECIES

They lusted for each other
like moon-struck lunatics
and acted upon it
before discussing it further.
Now, to their surprise and,
fortunately, short-lived horror,
they discover that shortly
she will be a proud mama
and he a doting papa.

And thus, my friend,
the human race began
and this, my friend,
guarantees angst without end
because babies grow up and,
like their mamas and papas,
become moon-struck lunatics
lusting for each other—
and then act upon it
before discussing it further.

LIFE

you
me
us
we
husband
wife
love
life
children
strife

LOVE (2/14/12)

I.   Love

a whetstone
of interlocking emotions
sharpening the senses

a caress
of the erotic smoothing
sharp corners and edges

a present
from the heart that liberates
the mind and soul

a mortgage
for adapting separate entities
into a unified whole

II.   Love

stretches the heart
opening it wide
to encompass the world
waiting outside

III.   Love

what the
heart believes
is truth

IV.   Love

a hummingbird
a juggernaut
a spring shower
a tsunami

V.   Love

exhilarating
habit forming stuff–
I've said enough.

THREE

Searching for morals, I seek
that woven between the lines,
hidden in the margins, lurking
among the laughs, the sighs, the cries.
I relish the poet's
rhythms, meters, and rhymes,
wrapping paper for the gift
of wonder found inside,
meantime absorbing, processing,
owning all the poet has said
and left unsaid—
now and forever mine.

PROMISE

His feet remembered the
thrill of races won;
his head remembered
the pride of aced exams;
his heart was full
of his first love;
his arm dreamed of throwing
the white orb to gold and fame;
his hands dreamed of dancing
over keyboards to world acclaim;
but all the same, disobeying
a direct order from his brain,
his finger pulled the trigger.

EDUCATION OF A BOY SOLDIER

When he was a child– not that long ago–
he lived in Nature, natural, as young
humans do, but too soon
Nurture tinkered with his reason,
rearranging synapses in his brain.

Socialized and civilized, he was taught
to serve his God and he was taught
to serve his State, but he was taught
to hate those who do not serve his
God and who do not serve his State.

Now each night he cleans his rifle
and rehearses his combat skill,
preparing for the next day's fight
and dreaming of his next kill.

METAMORPHOSIS

At age twenty-two he was
fueled by profuse infusions
of sugar and caffeine,
alcohol and nicotine,
ingesting beer by the liter,
inhaling cigarettes one after the other,
passionate about family,
country, and world politics,
a peacenik,
a star on the Liberal Team,
marching, protesting, writing letters
"To Whom It May Concern."
Hellbent on saving the world,
he was 100% pure content.

At age forty-eight he abstains
from sugar and nicotine and
has substituted wine for beer.
He sports a politician's smile
and a surgery-enhanced profile,
shaking hands, waving flags,
slapping and scratching backs,
kissing babies, loving the limelight.
A war hawk playing on the
Conservative Team, courting oil
companies and the Christian right,
claiming he is the American Way.
Hellbent on getting reelected,
he is 100% content free.

WHEN THE SUN FLAMED TOO HOT

when the sun flamed too hot
daddy flicked if off and lit the moon
or so I assumed

exploding bam! bam! bam!
air sprayed with daddy genome
daddy didn't bother coming home

vanished vanquished banished
can't hear can't see
can't breathe can't love me

wreckage from reckless love
nation duty adventure first
wife next daughter last

sing dissonance through
dried voice unpurified by tears
in a key no one hears

seas run slow run late
swimming between yes and no
and the undertow of limbo

wave a fan cool the sun
unfurl a parasol block the light
delay the moon postpone the night

exploding bam! bam! bam!
upheave bereave no reprieve
find something simpler to believe

ADORED

He was the adoring lover,
she, the adored,
at first lulled into thinking
she held the power
in their love alliance.

Conditioning her to breathe as he
directed, with one subtle maneuver
after another, he tilted her off balance.
She never knew just what would
anger or please her adoring lover.

Blindfolded by dependence, she
crept along a tightrope stretched
over a ravine, with each sliding
step fearful that her adoring lover
would withdraw his favors forever.

Then she made that minor misstep
that caused her lover to strike the blow
      that
      plunged
      her
      into
      the
      ravine
      below.

TO MAKE LIFE EASY

To make life easy he was advised
to omit needless things,
so he discarded his anchors
and lost his history.

To make life easy he was advised
to omit needless motions,
so he practiced inertia
and lost his mobility.

To make life easy he was advised
to omit needless words,
so he guarded his tongue
and lost his language.

To make life easy he was advised
to omit needless emotions,
so he hoarded his love
and lost human connections.

To make life easy he was advised
to omit needless thoughts,
but he did not heed this advice
since he could no longer think.

GREEN LIGHT

The child of vagabonds who
inhabit chemically enhanced
fogs, their souls scattering every

which way like autumn leaves,
she exists in storm clouds and
swampy midnight.   Famished

for prisms refracting rainbows,
thirsting for the honey dazzle
of sunshine, dreaming about

green freedom, yearning to be
rescued from the unlit prison
of storm clouds and swampy

midnight, she waits for an
invitation to sup and feast
in the garden of green light.

BEAUTY AT SIXTEEN

She tosses her long blonde hair,
widens her violet eyes,
smiles shyly– an unfurling flower
testing her feminine power.

From birth she has held her
dad and granddads spellbound.
Now at sixteen her cast
of potential admirers is vast.

In March she opens her arms
wide to receive the promise and
homage she considers due
her youth, charm, and beauty.

Who knows better than we older
women what can happen in April
when love and sexual attraction
demand her undivided attention.

ENCHANTMENT

If I cast a magic spell on the boy
I like by mixing an elixir for him
to imbibe, will it bind him to me by

opening his eyes to see the beauty
that is in me, so we can live in a
fairy tale epilogue of happily ever

after?   If the magic should dissipate,
thrusting him back to reality, and for
the first time he sees the real me,

will he not look back as he departs,
or will he stay to offer me clear and
free his unenchanted heart?   With

all these questions thrumming
through my head, I think it might
be easier to forget about the magic

elixir and just take a chance that
he is intelligent enough to see and
to want the rare jewel that is me.

Oh, yeah, like that's gonna happen.

FACEBOOK RELATIONSHIP

He posts: "I'm in a relationship!!!"
She posts: "I'm too happy for words!!!"
He swears he's hers.
She swears she's his.
His passion is infinite and electrifying.
Her love is forever and multiplying.

Two week later, she posts:
"He was like so lying.
But I'm through with all my crying.
And, get this– OMG!   I win.
I'm in a new relationship!!!"
Love-at-first-click oneupsmanship–

THE ELEPHANT IN THE ROOM

The beast lurks, crowding the corners,
commanding the center, too scorching
to seize, too wild to suppress.   It cannot

be ignored, concealed, nor tamed.
Merciless close ups and long takes
of crystallized scenes reveal sacrifices

of conscience, decisions to betray
love, to shatter truth, to flout the
conventions of a loving father.   The

addictive highs of chaos, drama, and
violence remaster the reels of prior
living into wastelands of sleepwalking

through tepid emotions.   The elephant
in the room becomes a pacing Bengal
tiger, untamed, uncaged, feeding on

raw, roller-coaster emotions and
growing fat on shame and guilt and
fear, a voracious beast that cannot be

ignored, contained, tamed, nor slain.

IN THE EYE

I write
about my grandparents, parents,
sister and brother, aunts and uncles,
cousins once, twice and thrice removed,
about the members of my family
inventing their lives
in whirlwinds of emotions and
in torrents of turbulent torque.

I include
the in-laws, the halves, the steps,
the fosters, and the adopted kin, who
have been seduced into the vortexes
of our spiraling family funnels.

I dreamed
when I was a child
that I was a changeling,
by chance a member of this family,
with no shared blood clotting between us,
related only by habit and love.

I evolved
by revolving from the eyes
of their dueling tornados to the edges.

I survive
in fertile grounds of shredded clouds,
attempting to write the stories
of their lives and mine in howling winds
and slashing rains with indelible ink
on soggy, disintegrating paper.

WEDDED TO RED CLAY

"I won't take your money, Son.
You worked too hard for it."
She was wedded to red clay, faithful,
never acquiescing,
ceding to neither push nor pull.

"Money isn't anything but money.
Can never be anything else,"
I quoted her.   She laughed.
"And I won't sell and move in with you.
I refuse to be a dependent crone clone."
I smiled, but the uncertainty of her
tomorrow cast shadows on my today.

Before I could recross her threshold,
the breeze that had been a whispered duet
between violin and flute crescendoed
to wind growling like a slide trombone.
Harp strings of lightning streaked the sky,
followed by trumpet peals of thunder,
rain wailing like a lonesome saxophone
against the tin roof.

We rocked on the porch, enjoying the
symphony, while I continued my futile
plea.   Wearing a clay smeared smock
spattered with the residue of achievements,
she smiled and shook her head.

As the symphony decrescendoed to the
soft plink-plink of a banjo, I knew that she
would die with arms embracing her life,
refusing to the end to relinquish red clay
or to become a clone.

STICKS AND STONES

Launching verbal grenades,
she screamed through life
on an oral rampage,
her empathy missing in action,
vanished without a trace.
She maimed the psyches of her
children with verbal barrages
that took no prisoners,
indifferent to the devastation
wreaked by bombardments
of oral artillery.

When called to account,
she shrugged and muttered,
>If I've offended them in any way,
>if I've caused them any distress,
>then I'm sorry,
as if her victims were responsible
for suffering the agony
her words inflicted.

In later years, sick with memories,
she sobbed,
>I'm so sorry.
However, nothing ever goes
back to normal simply because
someone says she's sorry.

LATE

Oh, shit– just look at the time.
It's gettin' late.
I need to be gettin' on home.
Oh, damn– I've missed the Kid's birthday.
Again.   I'll be in the doghouse for sure.
But, you know, uh, it's been a bitchin' party.
That last beer– well, it was great!
Uh– of course, I can drive.
No, don't try to take my keys.
No, I just– uh– I only had a couple–
I had a few beers.
My head's almost clear.
No need for you to worry.
I'm sober enough– just look, I can walk–
Oops– Well– I can– uh– I can
almost walk a straight line.
I can drive myself– my head's almost clear.
No need for you to– uh–
no need for you to worry.
I'll just call home– uh–
Sure, sure, I'll be all right.
I just need to call my kid.
Hey, Kid, it's me.
Your old man, that's who.
Sorry I missed your birthday, Kid.
I'll– uh– make it up to you, I swear.
Uh– no, no, nothing's wrong–
I'm just on my way home–
But tonight I'll be late–
No, no, don't wait–
It's just that tonight, Sweetie,
Tonight I'll be a little late.

THE PERFECT WOMAN*

From the age of twenty he has been
searching for the perfect woman who
matches his ideal of the perfect wife.
She will adore him, bear his children,
and serve him for the rest of his life.

First he dates one, and then he
dates another, only to discover that
one after the other is not the treasure
he requires in a wife because they all
fail to meet his exacting measure.

At last Grinning Fate leads him to his
perfect mate.   He concocts a courtship
campaign of dark chocolates and roses,
wining and dining, dancing, picnics, and
concerts.   Soon it's time he proposes.

He purchases a Princess Diana
sapphire and diamond ring, calls on
the perfect woman, kneels on one knee,
grabs her left hand and commands,
"Tell me that you'll marry me."

"No, no, no, absolutely not, no way,"
rejecting him, his ring, and his proposal,
she snatches back her ring-free hand.
"Thank you, but I cannot marry you.
I'm waiting for the perfect man."

*Based on a joke told me by former student, Chad
Chegwidden

SKIN DEEP

Short skirt
Sheer shirt
Face fair
Blonde hair
Pert breasts
Slim waist
Long legs–
He begs

Long skirt
Loose shirt
Face square
Drab hair
Flat chest
Thick waist
Fat knees–
He flees

FOUR

The poet's slanting sunbeams
blanket the world around me
with golden, translucent light,
warming the icy darkness
inside the freezing night.

LOCKED OUT

She counts her life in closed and
locked doors, standing outside,
heart in hand, afraid to knock,

tick-tock

scared to call, "Anyone home?" fearful
of hearing, "Go away," frightened
of being invited in should she knock,

tick-tock

but petrified most of all of being
ignored, snubbed, of receiving no
response at all to her timid knock,

tick-tock

locked out of the living teeming
on the other side, standing alone,
hope in hand, afraid to knock.

tick-tock
tick
tock

FUNERAL-WORTHY

I'm reading the obituaries, making notes
as I check on those who are now guests
of honor at our local funeral parlor,
determining who is funeral-worthy.
Today there are six candidates:

>Tony Todd, 78, my old school bus driver,
>a nice man, heart, visitation;
>
>Nellie McRae, 83, my eighth grade Sunday
>School teacher, an autocratic hypocrite,
>meanness, Dollar Store sympathy card;
>
>Nathan Canady, 75, a member of my church,
>a civic-minded man, cancer, covered dish;
>
>Della Hardin, 92, a member of my mother's
>bridge club, lovely lady, old age,
>flowers and funeral;
>
>Jim O'Toole, 58, ex-husband of a friend,
>a cheating jerk who left her for a floozy,
>cirrhosis, trip-to-hell ticket; and
>
>Mamie Lou Turner, 91, unknown to me,
>but the mother of a co-worker, stroke,
>donation in-lieu-of.

There! All checked and categorized—
only one funeral to attend.

"Honey, are you through with the comics yet?"

ALONE

Three women are whispering
at a table next to mine.
They do not whisper to me.

Three women are laughing
in the room next to mine.
I do not share their glee.

Three women are dining
in the kitchen next to mine.
They do not dine with me.

Three roses are blooming
in the garden next to mine.
They do not bloom for me.

Three robins are singing
in the tree next to mine.
I cannot heed their plea.

Three children are weeping
at the grave next to mine.
They do not weep for me.

PROCESS

Waterlogged, adrift in a frigid ocean,
I move in slow progression in a night,
stark and silent, sans the silver of the moon,

sans the golden promise of the dawning sun.
The sin of death hovers, a mere breath away.
I can smell land– pungent, alive–

distinguish it from clouds, breezes, waves.
To get to shore I need to imagine myself there.
The waves swirl and bend and I begin

to fall upwards from the depth of the sea.
Then I scrape bottom, drag myself ashore,
where jilted by the beauty of death, betrayed

by not finding God in every grain of sand,
I toss reason into the sun-lit air, defining
and refining the magic of the moment.

Tangled in then and now and what if, the
images drift and shift like tumbleweed
haunting the vacant streets of a ghost town.

Reacting to the cinema in my head, the nib
of my pen dips into the ink of my mind,
and I begin to write it all down.

BLIND CORNERS

With emptiness threatening to devour us,
our trio sped through stop signs,
careened around blind corners, and
drove the wrong way across one-way bridges.

Heading for something we didn't want,
trying to be something we didn't want to be,
revving up the engine—faster—faster—faster
as we kept asking, "If not here, where?"

Fatigued by our mothers' dreams,
we shipped our nightmares around the globe,
but our brains kept shedding cells from
hanging upside down avoiding the expected.

Then home became more than an address, so
we returned home, threw open the windows,
and reconciled with our mothers,
who knew us before we wore bras.

The people we saw and places we visited
were bigger, more exotic, than ourselves.
Seeping into our sunburnt pores,
they became our temporary reality.

But, did we grow and did we change?
Ha! We just became more of the same.
Now, we whip froth into miniature rainbows
and mine our past for anecdotes and laughs.

A SWORD OF ROSES

Half-way through a novel I find plotless,
the characters only intermittently
interesting, giving no shape to the
shapelessness of being, I start speed
reading, skipping descriptions and
expositions, asking, "Where's the truth?"

I invent new plot lines about love in
mid-life with its dangers of integration
and contention, turn love into a sword of
roses, splice in obscure symbols and
motifs, refine universal themes, and
introduce a handsome, savior-hero.

The heroine does not need saving,
except from herself.   Thus, I create
ephemeral happiness born of unfounded
optimism while avoiding flashes of
softened flesh bared in the fading beauty
of mid-years— before turning out the light.

I emerge, nose pressed against the
glass, my mind drugged with ink and
milling with characters found at family
reunions and funeral parlors, drying from
the complications of disappointment
with a journey that never reaches spring.

The reviewers promised so much more.

BOOM!

With my mother's milk I started to absorb
a set of unvoiced rules.   The rules
descended on me, a net morphing into a cage.

As long as I stayed within the cage, creating
a framework of diligence and propriety and
an outward obeisance, no one, nothing would

harm me.   Sometimes something undefined,
unarticulated, overwhelmed me.   Having
a primeval instinct for survival, I choose

not to travel alone, even if I was just a
shadow in the edges of others' eyes, and
even though other humans were a nuisance

and exhausted me.   Then my cage was
wrenched from me, vanquished by the thing.
The thing that filled the resulting vacuum,

an unnamed presence, giving me a sense of
secret power, making my covert world loud
and shrill, festered in the dank cellar of my

psyche, holding a smoldering cigarette
to a fuse. Then one day it all went BOOM!
It's good to be done with things.

AND THE ROAD CURVES ON

Begging to escape the Demon's thrall
and to end her dependence ordeal,
she searches for a sanctuary,
a place to hide and to heal.

But the wheels spin round
and the road curves on—

Yearning for that elusive Utopia
where she can atone for all her sins,
she prays for the wheels to stop
and pleads for the road to end.

But the wheels spin round and round
and the road curves on and on—

THE TEXTURE OF HOPE

Confronted by echoing emptiness
as the house creaked and groaned,
adjusting to a new order
in the silence of oneness, I saw my
days and nights gaping wide open.

Running away to a secluded beach
to escape the echoing oneness,
I stalled in deep water as two-by-two
all others sailed past me
going in the opposite direction.

I struggled to flip over from a
dead-man's-float, releasing myself
from crushing fears and
drowning doubts as I battled
to reach shore.   Back home,

I ran my fingers through
the texture of hope,
rewound the clocks,
and pruned the dead fronds
from the ferns.

KEEP IT SIMPLE

I'm busy; don't philosophize.
Use words I can comprehend
and keep it simple so I can
pretend to understand.

Don't give me the provenance
of that piece of art or antique;
just inform me that it is,
without a doubt, unique.

Don't expound on our
involvement in Afghanistan,
explain why we can't win in Iraq,
and why we lost in Viet Nam.

Don't pontificate at length
on the physics of the universe;
just tell me in simple terms
how we can save our Earth.

No time to delve deep, but
sound bites distort information,
so keep the message simple and
give me an in-depth summation.

STANDING ALONE IN THE RAIN

Why is that person standing alone in the rain?
Fists clenched, crying and inconsolable.
Why is that person waiting alone for a train?
Greeting no one and unknowable.

Why is that person walking alone on the beach?
Head bowed, stumbling and unreachable.
Why is that person sailing alone on the sea?
Shrouded in fog and unfathomable.

Why is that person dining alone in her home?
Drowning in ice and unquenchable.
Why is that person sleeping alone in her room?
In a bed, sterile and stark and impregnable.

Why is that person walking alone in the park?
At midnight, cold and dark and untouchable.
Why am I standing alone in the rain?
Palms outstretched, asking and unanswerable.

BOTTLED PROMISES

Measuring life in proof percentages
and in shot glasses of liquid Sirens,
she is seduced by the ruby red and
bewitched by the diamond white.

The first drink enables her to create
a persona— charming, witty, bright;
the second drink burnishes the
performance to a sparkling luster.

The third drink tenders her a revised
history, strength, and succor;
the fourth begins as her psychologist
and replaces her priest and confessor.

The fifth becomes her commerce
her art, her faith, her destiny;
the sixth steals her wisdom and virtue
and ousts her family, friends, and goals.

The seventh liquid Siren, bottled in
amber light teeming with counterfeit
promises, blinds her instincts,
shatters her life, and damns her soul.

ALLOW ME MY ANGER, PLEASE

Allow me my anger, please.
You've taken my joy, my peace,
my trust in humanity.
If you leave me with nothing else,
let me keep and cultivate my anger.

Let me cherish it with obsession,
nurture it with tears, and
fertilize it with sleepless nights.
Let me root out competing emotions,
and mulch it with resentment.

Let me watch over it so
it will flourish and crowd out
my regrets, my disappointments,
my pain, my grief, my sorrow.
So at least until the morrow,

Let me feast on my anger.   Please.

THE MYSTERY OF THE PEA

Who put that small pea under my mattress?
I'm black; I'm blue; I am ugly as sin.
I'd like to slip the guilty culprit a
poisoned apple from my step-mother's bin.
I still feel the pain from that baby pea.

This morning I can't find any fresh
golden eggs.   My goose had lost her charge.
The glass slippers my fairy godmother
Elf-Exed to me are two sizes too large.
I am still aching from that tiny pea.

Next, I get warts from kissing a frog.
Instead of gold from flax, I spin linen,
and my tresses have developed split ends.
Right now that evil culprit is winnin'.
Oh, the agony of that little pea!

A big, bad wolf comes howling and prowling,
huffing and puffing outside my stick house,
and my evil step-mother has cast a spell
to conceal her golden apples.   The louse!
All my woes began with that petite pea.

No golden egg is my goose laying;
that croaking frog has given me warts;
the big, bad wolf is huffing and puffing;
my hair is frizzy; I'm all out of sorts.
Who put that nasty pea under my mattress?

All the clues lead directly to the Queen,
mother of that fat, pompous prince.
I hope she does not expect the two of us
to fall in love and live happily ever since.
But she did put that pea under my mattress.

ONE PERFECT PANCAKE GRIDDLE

On Christmas Day my true-love gave to me
one perfect cast-iron pancake griddle.
Tenderly his expectations he made clear:
pancakes with blueberries in the middle.
He demanded full value for the gift
of that perfect pancake griddle.

One perfect vacuum cleaner for an anniversary,
a mower for my birthday, plus, Happy Yuletide!,
for Christmas that flippin' pancake griddle–
all encouraged me to ponder, then decide,
after consulting Merriam-Webster,
how to commit the perfect mariticide.

Ms. Parker yearned for one perfect limousine,
instead she received one perfect rose.
Now, I'm here to tell you in rhyming sestets,
if I were so lucky, I wouldn't turn up my nose
at a lover who on Christmas Day gave to me
one flippin' perfect rose.

ODE TO WINE

O, Nectar from the grape, Nature's gift,
you alleviate hobbling anxiety,
are a stress-reducer, a social lubricant,
and you palliate old-age infirmity.

With a golden angst-conquering glow,
you generate widespread conviviality,
and you are a potable comfort and joy
guaranteed to eradicate sobriety.

FIVE

The poet has the power to conjure
colors so that all else fades,
to spin straw into gold and then
weave it into poems rife with fairy dust
designed to illuminate and to deceive.
But– what matter if truths be lies
or lies be truths as long as I believe?

QUARTET

I.   INTERRUPTED

Under the unlit crystal chandelier
the mahogany dining room table hosts
one thousand jig-saw puzzle pieces.

A glimmer of fading sunlight tiptoes
through the apple orchard and briefly
illuminates the box lid's forest scene

in myriad shades of blue and green.
Four pushed back chairs stand empty,
but at each place a corner of the puzzle

has been fitted together.
A film of dust has nestled on and
among the puzzle pieces, separated

into varying shades of blue and green,
and has coated the box lid's forest scene.
The candles on the mahogany buffet

have burnt and spilt over the edges
of the silver candlesticks, a valedictory
in a room reeking with the agony

of unanswered why's.

QUARTET

II.   MORNING

Rain has fallen all night
in hushed whispers of silent tears.
More tears are in the clouds

waiting in the quiet of first light.
Ghostly mist hovers over the lake, and
gray fog shrouds the hillside orchard,

the grass below frosted white.
Lamps will stay lit this morning
in an attempt to banish the dark

as black, as opaque as anthracite,
in an attempt to ignite healing
in a home still reeling, still mourning

an abruptly extinguished light.

QUARTET

III.   NECKLACE OF TEARS

My life thudded and shattered
into minute pieces too slivery
to be glued back together, and I

began stringing a necklace of tears.
My voice fragmented,
sharp shards by-passing the ears

of sympathetic listeners.
I replayed endlessly the dull thud,
the sharp splintering, accompanied

by my broken cries of loss as I
strung one tear after another.
I longed to sleep with you again

in our marriage bed; I dreamed of
joining you on your funeral pyre.
When will I finish stringing

my necklace of tears?

QUARTET

IV.   COMING IN FROM THE DARK

While you were with me, I lived too much in
the misty margins between sleep and dreams,
ruled by seasons of small reason.

Caught up in the dailiness of life, I worried
about the mundane, the seldom relished,
gliding past the joy of the moment.

Days, weeks, months, seasons passed
as I wove loose patterns between the years.
Most years split seamlessly

into four equal parts.   After your leaving
I lived through an endless winter that bled
the joy from longer and longer days.

In the slanted amber light of late afternoon
I watch our grandson quarterbacking his last
college football game, his girlfriend cheering.

Your memory lives in him and as I watch,
I relive the legend of our youth–
Friday night high school football games,

chrysanthemum corsages and kisses
worth the granting whether you won or lost.
It's time for me to come in from the dark.

I've finished stringing my necklace of tears.

MISS LILY'S FUNERAL

Wrapped in pink, frilly nylon,
Miss Lily is packed
into her deluxe mahogany casket,
lined in tufted pastel blue satin,
like a doll displayed in a gift box.

An environmentalist,
Miss Lily had specified recycled pine.
Miss Lily hated synthetics;
she despised pink frills,
and she wasn't thrilled by tufts either.

Clutching the pulpit and in beats of four
rising on tiptoe, the preacher,
who has never met Miss Lily,
intones generic platitudes,
labeling her a good Christian woman,
a loving daughter, wife, and mother,
tabulating nothing connected
to Miss Lily's full-throttle life.

Miss Lily had little use for most
ministers and abhorred funerals, which
she never attended when she was alive.

The preacher has no clue that Miss Lily
thought it paradoxical that she had
a burdening sense of sin without the
religious beliefs to assuage guilt
with forgiveness and absolution.

Miss Lily had requested cremation–
no viewing, no funeral, no open casket–
and a joyous celebration of her life.
She included the directions in her will.

Her daughter, a contrarian from birth,
for which Miss Lily blamed herself,
has never genetically validated her mother.
She is sending Miss Lily to the Hereafter
with an open-casket funeral where
the robed choir sings ponderous hymns.

Miss Lily was insulted by old age,
but she had no fear of that long silence
of ultimate negativity that follows dying.
A reader and a gardener, she requested,
"In lieu of flowers, make a contribution
to your local library."

She is surrounded by wreaths of
artistically arranged decaying glads.
Miss Lily would not allow a gladiolus
corm-room in her herbaceous borders.

We who loved Miss Lily are twice bereft–
at her exit and at her daughter's
latest and final betrayal.

ANGEL OF MERCY

When the sky falls,
there are pieces to pick up
and glue back together,
a need to be up and busy at daybreak,
wounds to suture and bandage,
psyches to soothe and spirits to raise,
casseroles to assemble and cakes to bake,
beds to strip and then remake,
places to go and trouble to take,
broken hearts and fences to mend,
and maybe
a funeral to help arrange and attend.

When the sky doesn't fall,
when her immediate world
is turmoil and worry free,
floating on breezes of happiness,
she secretly yearns
for the sky to fall so there is a need
to be up and busy at daybreak
and there are beds to strip and remake,
casseroles to assemble and cakes to bake,
broken hearts and relationships to mend,
and if she's lucky,
a funeral to arrange and attend.

BITTER WEEDS AND ROSES

How many times did the sun beat down
burning the grass a brittle brown
and then gently urge it to green again
while Penelope awaited her Ulysses?

Risque and politically incorrect toasts and
jokes fill the ballroom with a merry uproar.
The celebrated couple runs from a shower
of champagne into the refuge of dry martinis.

Lips positioned to imitate pleasure,
her heart flutters to and fro like the wings
of a captured ruby-throated hummingbird.
Happy to forgo the life she has endured

But reluctant to forfeit the liberty enjoyed
during her husband's tours of duty,
she aches from the festivities, from smiling.
The smile falters, begins to decay.

Bereft of regimentation, adventure,
the company of men, he stands at ease,
arm draped over her shoulder.
Death wasn't as heroic as Homer depicted.

It was often just a minute misstep, a lapse,
an if. The names of the dead scroll
through his head, a video permanently
stuck on play, looping, looping, looping.

Their union has always been a path lined
with bitter weeds and roses. Yet– maybe
love will flourish anew if the sun can
nourish the grass to green again. Maybe–

THE WHEEL OF TIME

Tumbling inside the Wheel of Time—

nineteen—

Wishing, wanting, dreaming—

twenty-nine—

I was meant for something great.
The world would know my face,
call me by my first name.
My talents and my life would unfurl
on a wide-screen landscape.

thirty-nine—

High of heart
I would dance the lead in SWAN LAKE,
or take fifteen curtain calls in the role
of Rosalind in AS YOU LIKE IT,
or play a duel with that Russian pianist
at Carnegie Hall,
or sing AIDA at the Met.

forty-nine—

Whichever talent I'd choose to use,
I'd win awards, honors, accolades,
and get high on affirming applause.

fifty-nine—

I was meant for something great.
My talents should have unfurled
on a wide-screen landscape.

sixty-nine–

Tumbling inside the Wheel of Time–

seventy-nine–

MISSING KEY

Last chances flicker past as I
drive on fog-shrouded back roads
searching for the missing key
that will open the locked gate
to the copse of sacred trees blessed
with twenty-one angles of light.

Driving alone on uncharted roads,
I am a quixotic seeker
from nowhere going no place,
but going there in panic and haste
while happiness flees from me
like the dark before my headlamps.

In the deep crevices of my mind
where nightmares lurk and
demons wear masks,
I know my life is brick-walled,
resistant to the story of another's
life, and that the key I seek
will open no gate wide enough
for love to edge through.

OLD MAN TIME, THE THIEF

Old Man Time, the Thief,
impolite– he had no invitation–
broke into my life at midnight.
He stooped my straight back,
robbing me of valuable height,
etched wrinkles on my face,
and dimmed my eyesight.

He bagged under my eyes,
dulled my acute hearing,
streaked gray through my mane,
muddied my clear complexion,
varicosed my leg veins,
sagged my taut neck, and
befuddled my keen brain.

He laughed at my objections.
Then, with belated generosity,
he bestowed a birthright.
In lieu of his purloined loot
he gave me a bit of foresight,
just a smidgen of insight,
and twenty-twenty hindsight.

He sniggered as he swaggered
toward the splintered back door.
"Stop your bitching.   Forsooth!
I'll be back tomorrow night
prepared, to tell you the truth,
to steal more of your beauty,
your vigor, and your youth."

WEAVING NETS TO CATCH THE WIND

The illusion behind the reflection,
hoarded images of the me that used
to be, contradicts the reality I see

in the mirror.   The mind can deny
the consequences of Time's rotating
progression by eluding the visible,

by rejecting alterations of substance,
by weaving nets, though progressive
change is a mugger slugging me

in the face. Until the day my vanity
is sucked dry to satisfy the indifferent
rotations of Greedy Time, I'll continue

weaving nets to catch the wind.

SHE FEELS THE FUTURE

Up the stairs she once sped
taking two steps at a time
and then pranced down them
like a Kentucky thoroughbred.
She never touched the hand rails.
Now she keeps a death hold
and she rests on each tread,
stoic to the torture
in feet, ankles, and knees.
She is filled with dread,
uncertainty in each step,
as she feels the future
with each hard-won tread.

Her middle-aged children
hold their breaths in concern
and worry that in too few years
it will be their turn.

SENSIBLE SHOES

When did she become that woman
inhabiting sensible shoes
and elastic-waisted slacks,
wearing liver-colored lipstick?

When did she stop caring
that men and women dance to the music
of the universe in different beats,
and when did she stop flirting
with the clash and sizzle of dissonance?

Time pulsed when she basked
in the sunshine of clash and sizzle,
dining on caviar and champagne,
sporting black lace lingerie, short skirts,
high-heeled slings, dangling ear rings,
showcasing carmine lips and nails,
embracing a hand with four aces–
a royal tern soaring over a barrier island,
a butterfly nectaring in a quilted meadow,
a palomino galloping through morning mist,
a mermaid tangoing beneath a rainbow's arc–

Now time limps as she sits and sips broth,
dressed for a funeral, zero for a mouth.

THE PLAY'S THE THING

I've blundered onto the stage
in the middle of Act Two,
unaware of the plot and
characters introduced and
developed earlier in the play,
not knowing how to act,
not knowing what to say.
Have I stumbled into the midst
of a farce or a mystery?
a romance or a history?

What is my role? My motivation?
Is it true that the audience
will turn thumbs down
if I miss one cue?
I wish I knew what happened
in Act One and what
will happen in Act Three.
Busy bluffing my way through
the remainder of Act Two,
I have no clue.

As the second act ends and the
third begins, I'm wagering my
life on never missing a mark,
never missing a line,
guessing at one cue at a time.
I'm steeling myself to expect
nothing at the end of the play
but praying that I'll receive
a standing ovation,
shouts of "Bravo! Bravo!"
and a bouquet of Peace roses
when the final curtain closes.

RACING

I ran just beyond His reach,
His icy whispers scorching my ears,
igniting my primordial fears.
I raced through my lows, my highs,
fleeing through the days, the nights,
the seasons of the years.

I fled from Him
down labyrinthine paths,
through primeval forests
and intricate mazes,
on serpentine trails and
up precipitous mountains,
across mesas, oceans, deserts,
up the Amazon,
down the Nile,
across the Mississippi,
up and down impatient city streets,
sleepy country lanes, and around
sand dunes on tide washed beaches–
He chasing– I racing
just beyond His frigid reaches.

But–
He is stronger, swifter, surer.
In the end I'll not outpace
His eternal embrace.
But, oh the joy, the jubilation
of the race!

ADVANCE WARNING

O.K., Death, I'm warning you,
if you want me,
you'll have to come get me,
but you'll need two battalions
of demon knights mounted
on stalwart war stallions
to help you vanquish me.

I dare you to come
on a wild, stormy night with
lighting flashing,
thunder crashing,
wind shrieking,
rain slashing,
and wolves howling.

I've lived wild and I've lived free;
the furies of my soul will ride with
me as I go kicking and screaming
and swearing, shaking my fists
in your malignant face.
I'm warning you, Death,
I'll fight you unto my final breath.

IS IT SPRING YET?

It is obvious to the discerning eye
that what is broken cannot be mended.
My life has not been a sentence
that can be diagramed, but it is
a sentence in need of a period
as it approaches its ending.

I ponder the best season to die,
weighing the pros and cons of each.
I leave the door to my heart ajar, hoping
the backlog of sorrows will creep out
and prodigal memories will tiptoe back in
while the waiting curtains billow and snap.

I would like to repose
in the heart of my chosen season,
in the core of its memories, swirling down
into its vortex as my soul prepares
to slip into an infant as she sails
head first down her mother's birth canal.

Is it spring yet?

INEXACT

You were with me
at the beginning of spring.
We raced the hare,
lived verdant, inexact.

Now you are with me
at the end of winter.
We whisper to the tortoise
we are slower than he.

And it was all a fragment
of an inexact moment.

EPILOGUE

Is there a happy ending?
The Universe has not informed me
since my story continues to unfold–
not just my own biography,
but the saga of the evolving,
persistent world, a continuum
with or without me–
neither good nor evil, just
supremely indifferent– leaving
me to make of it what I may
as I write and act my own drama–
both tragic and comic–
seeking to give my existence
substance and purpose–
and joy.

ACKNOWLEDGMENTS

I wish to thank the following people:

Dianne Cox, Donna Spivey, Claire Stewart, Shelly Murphy, Joy Padgett, Bob Covell, and David Crowe for suggestions and corrections; the Carrollton Creative Writers Club for support; Diana Black for the cover design of DRIVING WITH MY BLINKER ON; the members of Just Poetry Workshop for their incredible insights; Penny Lewis for her support of the arts; Angelia Hoomes for editing and technical assistance; John Bell, my patient publisher; Wendell Hoomes, who likes the humorous poems; and the readers of my previous volumes of poetry for their insights and encouragements.

www.ingramcontent.com/pod-product-compliance
Lightning Source LLC
Chambersburg PA
CBHW072006060426
42446CB00042B/2001